Dear Young People

PUBLISHER'S NOTE

The texts of the addresses and homilies of Pope Benedict XVI contained in this booklet are the official texts released by the Vatican Press Office. During his actual delivery, the Holy Father occasionally left out a sentence or phrase, possibly inadvertently or for reasons of time and, on other occasions, added a spontaneous comment. However, the Vatican Press Office has advised that, for the record, 'the official text is taken as read'. Accordingly, the publishers of this volume have made no attempt to adjust the texts to incorporate any slight variations in the Pope's spoken delivery.

Pope Benedict XVI leads the congregation in prayer during the World Youth Day Mass in Sydney.

Dear Young People

Homilies and Addresses of

POPE BENEDICT XVI

Apostolic Journey to Sydney, Australia
on the occasion of the
23rd World Youth Day
12 to 21 July 2008

ST PAULS

DEAR YOUNG PEOPLE: Homilies and Addresses of Pope Benedict XVI. Apostolic Journey to Sydney, Australia, on the occasion of the 23rd World Youth Day, 12 to 21 July 2008

This edition published with the approval of the Australian Catholic Bishops Conference.

First published, 2008

National Library of Australia
Card Number and ISBN 978 1 921472 14 5

Published by
ST PAULS PUBLICATIONS
PO Box 906
Strathfield NSW 2135 Australia
www.stpauls.com.au

Cover photo courtesy of *The Catholic Weekly*
www.worldyouthday08-photos.com.au
All other photos by Ivàn de Vargas.
Reproduced with permission.

Cover design and layout by Kylie Prats
Printed by Ligare Pty Ltd

ST PAULS PUBLICATIONS is an activity of the priests and brothers of the Society of St Paul who place at the centre of their lives the mission of evangelisation through the means of social communication.

Contents

1

Welcoming Ceremony

Government House, Sydney
Thursday, 17 July 2008

Your Excellencies,
Dear Australian Friends,

It is with great joy that I greet you today. I would like to thank the Governor-General, Major-General Michael Jeffery and Prime Minister Rudd for honouring me by their presence at this ceremony and for welcoming me so graciously. As you know, I have been able to enjoy some quiet days since my arrival in Australia last Sunday. I am most grateful for the hospitality that has been extended to me. Now I look forward to this evening's "Welcome to Country" by the indigenous people and to celebrating the great events which form the purpose of my Apostolic Visit: the Twenty-Third World Youth Day.

Some might ask what motivates thousands of young people to undertake what is for many a long and demanding journey in order to participate in an event of this kind. Ever since the first World Youth Day in 1986, it has been evident that vast numbers of young people appreciate the opportunity to come together to deepen their faith in Christ and to share with one another a joyful experience of communion in his

Church. They long to hear the word of God, and to learn more about their Christian faith. They are eager to take part in an event which brings into focus the high ideals that inspire them, and they return home filled with hope and renewed in their resolve to contribute to the building of a better world. For me it is a joy to be with them, to pray with them and to celebrate the Eucharist with them. World Youth Day fills me with confidence for the future of the Church and the future of our world.

It seems particularly appropriate to celebrate World Youth Day here, since the Church in Australia, as well as being the youngest of any continent, is also one of the most cosmopolitan. Since the first European settlement here in the late eighteenth century, this country has become a home not only to generations of Europeans, but to people from every corner of the globe. The immense diversity of the Australian population today gives a particular vibrancy to what may still be considered, in comparison with much of the rest of the world, a young nation. Yet for thousands of years before the arrival of Western settlers, the sole inhabitants of the land were indigenous peoples, the Aborigines and Torres Strait Islanders. Their ancient heritage forms an essential part of the cultural landscape of modern Australia. Thanks to the Australian Government's courageous decision to acknowledge the injustices committed against the indigenous peoples in the past, concrete steps are now being taken to achieve reconciliation based on mutual respect. Rightly, you are seeking to close the gap between indigenous and non-indigenous Australians regarding life expectancy, educational achievement and economic opportunity! This example of reconciliation offers hope to peoples all over the world who long to see their rights affirmed and their contribution to society acknowledged and promoted.

The settlers who came here from Europe have always included a significant proportion of Catholics, and we may be justly proud of the contribution they have made to the building up of the nation, particularly in the fields of education and healthcare. One of the most outstanding figures in this country's history is Blessed Mary MacKillop, at whose tomb I shall pray later this morning. I know that her perseverance in the face of adversity, her plea for justice on behalf of those unfairly treated and her practical example of holiness have become a source of inspiration for all Australians. Generations have reason to be grateful to her and to the Sisters of Saint Joseph of the Sacred Heart and other religious congregations for the network of schools that they established here and for the witness of their consecrated life. In today's more secular environment, the Catholic community continues to make an important contribution to national life, not only through education and healthcare, but especially by highlighting the spiritual dimension of the questions that feature prominently in contemporary debate.

With many thousands of young people visiting Australia at this time, it is appropriate to reflect upon the kind of world we are handing on to future generations. In the words of your national anthem, this land "abounds in nature's gifts, of beauty rich and rare". The wonder of God's creation reminds us of the need to protect the environment and to exercise responsible stewardship of the goods of the earth. In this connection I note that Australia is making a serious commitment to address its responsibility to care for the natural environment. Likewise with regard to the human environment, this country has generously supported international peace-keeping operations, contributing to conflict resolution in the Pacific, in South-East Asia and elsewhere. Owing to the many religious traditions represented in Australia, this is particularly fertile ground for ecumenical and interreligious dialogue. I look forward to meeting local representatives of different Christian communities and other religions during my stay, so as to encourage this important work, a sign of the reconciling action of the Spirit who impels us to seek unity in truth and charity.

First and foremost, though, I am here to meet the young, from Australia and from all over the world, and to pray for a renewed outpouring of the Holy Spirit upon all those taking part in our celebrations. The theme chosen for World Youth Day 2008 is taken from words spoken by Jesus himself to his disciples, as recorded in the Acts of the Apostles: "You shall receive power when the Holy Spirit has come upon you, and you shall be my witnesses to the ends of the earth" (1:9). I pray that the Holy Spirit will bring spiritual renewal to this land, to the Australian people, to the Church throughout Oceania and indeed to the ends of the earth. Young people today face a bewildering variety of life-choices, so that they sometimes find it hard to know how best to channel their idealism and their energy. It is the Spirit who gives the wisdom to discern the right path and the courage to follow it. He crowns our poor efforts with his divine gifts, just as the wind filling the sails sweeps the ship forward, far surpassing what the oarsmen can achieve through their laborious rowing. In this way, the Spirit enables men and women in every land and in every generation to become saints. Through the Spirit's action, may the young people gathered here for World Youth Day have the courage to become saints! This is what the world needs more than anything else.

Dear Australian friends, once again I thank you for your generous welcome and I look forward to spending these days with you and with the young people of the world. May God bless all who are present, all the pilgrims and all who live in this land. And may he always bless and protect the Commonwealth of Australia.

2

Welcoming Celebration by the Young People

Barangaroo, Sydney Harbour
Thursday, 17 July 2008

Dear Young People,

What a delight it is to greet you here at Barangaroo, on the shores of the magnificent Sydney harbour, with its famous bridge and Opera House. Many of you are local, from the outback or the dynamic multicultural communities of Australian cities. Others of you have come from the scattered islands of Oceania, and others still from Asia, the Middle East, Africa and the Americas. Some of you, indeed, have come from as far as I have, Europe! Wherever we are from, we are here at last in Sydney. And together we stand in our world as God's family, disciples of Christ, empowered by his Spirit to be witnesses of his love and truth for everyone!

I wish firstly to thank the Aboriginal Elders who welcomed me prior to my boarding the boat at Rose Bay. I am deeply moved to stand on your land, knowing the suffering and injustices it has borne, but aware too of the healing and hope that are now at work, rightly bringing pride to all Australian citizens. To the young indigenous – Aboriginal and Torres Strait Islanders – and the Tokelauans, I express my thanks for your stirring welcome. Through you, I send heartfelt greetings to your peoples.

Cardinal Pell and Archbishop Wilson, I thank you for your warm words of welcome. I know that your sentiments resonate in the hearts of the young gathered here this evening, and so I thank you all. Standing before me I see a vibrant image of the universal Church. The variety of nations and cultures from which you hail shows that indeed Christ's Good News is for everyone; it has reached the ends of the earth. Yet I know too that a good number of you are still seeking a spiritual homeland. Some of you, most welcome among us, are not Catholic or Christian. Others of you perhaps hover at the edge of parish and Church life. To you I wish to offer encouragement: step forward into Christ's loving embrace; recognize the Church as your home. No one need remain on the outside, for from the day of Pentecost the Church has been one and universal.

This evening I wish also to include those who are not present among us. I am thinking especially of the sick or mentally ill, young people in prison, those struggling on the margins of our societies, and those who for whatever reason feel alienated from the Church. To them I say: Jesus is close to you! Feel his healing embrace, his compassion and mercy!

Almost two thousand years ago, the Apostles, gathered in the upper room together with Mary and some faithful women, were filled with the Holy Spirit (cf. *Acts* 1:14; 2:4). At that extraordinary moment, which gave birth to the Church, the confusion and fear that had gripped Christ's disciples were transformed into a vigorous conviction and sense of purpose. They felt impelled to speak of their encounter with the risen Jesus whom they had come to call affectionately, the Lord. In many ways, the Apostles were ordinary. None could claim to be the perfect disciple. They failed to recognize Christ (cf. *Lk* 24:13-32), felt ashamed of their own ambition (cf. *Lk* 22:24-27), and had even denied him (cf. *Lk* 22:54-62). Yet, when empowered by the Holy Spirit, they were transfixed by the truth of Christ's Gospel and inspired to proclaim it fearlessly. Emboldened, they exclaimed: repent, be baptized, receive the Holy Spirit (cf. *Acts* 2:37-38)! Grounded in the Apostles' teaching, in fellowship, and in the breaking of the bread and prayer (cf. *Acts* 2:42), the young Christian community moved forward to oppose the perversity in the culture around them (cf. *Acts* 2:40), to care for one another (cf. *Acts* 2:44-47), to defend their belief in Jesus in the face of hostility (cf *Acts* 4:33), and to heal the sick (cf. *Acts* 5:12-16). And in obedience to Christ's own command, they set forth, bearing witness to the greatest story ever: that God has become one of us, that the divine has entered human history in order to transform it, and that we are called to immerse ourselves in Christ's saving love which triumphs over evil and death. Saint Paul, in his famous speech to the Areopagus, introduced the message in this way: "God gives everything – including life and breath – to everyone … so that all nations might seek God and, by feeling their way towards him, succeed in finding him. In fact he is not far from any of us, since it is in him that we live and move and have our being" (*Acts* 17: 25-28).

And ever since, men and women have set out to tell the same story, witnessing to Christ's truth and love, and contributing to the Church's mission. Today, we think of those pioneering Priests, Sisters and Brothers who came to these shores, and to other parts of the Pacific, from Ireland, France, Britain and elsewhere in Europe. The great majority were young – some still in their late teens – and when they bade farewell to their parents, brothers and sisters, and friends, they knew they were unlikely ever to return home. Their whole lives were a selfless Christian witness. They became the humble but tenacious builders of so much of the social and spiritual heritage which still today brings goodness, compassion and purpose to these nations. And they went on to inspire another generation. We think immediately of the faith which sustained Blessed Mary MacKillop in her sheer determination to educate especially the poor, and Blessed Peter To Rot in his steadfast resolution that community leadership must always include the Gospel. Think also of your own grandparents and parents, your first teachers in faith. They too have made countless sacrifices of time and energy, out of love for you. Supported by your parish priests and teachers, they have the task, not always easy but greatly satisfying, of guiding you towards all that is good and true, through their own witness – their teaching and living of our Christian faith.

Today, it is my turn. For some of us, it might seem like we have come to the end of the world! For people of your age, however, any flight is an exciting prospect. But for me, this one was somewhat daunting! Yet the views afforded of our planet from the air were truly wondrous. The sparkle of the Mediterranean, the grandeur of the north African desert, the lushness of Asia's forestation, the vastness of the Pacific Ocean, the horizon upon which the sun rose and set, and the majestic splendour of Australia's natural beauty which I have been able to enjoy these last couple of days; these all evoke a profound sense of awe. It is as though one catches glimpses of the Genesis creation story – light and darkness, the sun and the moon, the waters, the earth, and living creatures; all of which are "good" in God's eyes (cf. *Gen* 1:1 – 2:4). Immersed in such beauty, who could not echo the words of the Psalmist in praise of the Creator: "how majestic is your name in all the earth?" (*Ps* 8:1).

And there is more – something hardly perceivable from the sky – men and women, made in nothing less than God's own image and likeness (cf. *Gen* 1:26). At the heart of the marvel of creation are you and I, the human family "crowned with glory and honour" (*Ps* 8:5). How astounding! With the Psalmist we whisper: "what is man that you are mindful of him?" (*Ps* 8:4). And drawn into silence, into a spirit of thanksgiving, into the power of holiness, we ponder.

What do we discover? Perhaps reluctantly we come to acknowledge that there are also scars which mark the surface of our earth: erosion, deforestation, the squandering of the world's mineral and ocean resources in order to fuel an insatiable consumption. Some of you come from island nations whose very existence is threatened by rising water levels; others from nations suffering the effects of devastating drought. God's wondrous creation is sometimes experienced as almost hostile to its stewards, even something dangerous. How can what is "good" appear so threatening?

And there is more. What of man, the apex of God's creation? Every day we encounter the genius of human achievement. From advances in medical sciences and the wise application of technology, to the creativity reflected in the arts, the quality and enjoyment of people's lives in many ways are steadily rising. Among yourselves there is a readiness to take up the plentiful opportunities offered to you. Some of you excel in studies, sport, music, or dance and drama, others of you have a keen sense of social justice and ethics, and many of you take up service and voluntary work. All of us, young and old, have those moments when the innate goodness of the human person – perhaps glimpsed in the gesture of a little child or an adult's readiness to forgive – fills us with profound joy and gratitude.

Yet such moments do not last. So again, we ponder. And we discover that not only the natural but also the social environment – the habitat we fashion for ourselves – has its scars; wounds indicating that something is amiss. Here too, in our personal lives and in our communities, we can encounter a hostility, something dangerous; a poison which threatens to corrode what is good, reshape who we are, and distort the purpose for which we have been created. Examples abound, as you yourselves know. Among the more prevalent are alcohol and drug abuse, and the exaltation of violence and sexual degradation, often presented through television and the internet as entertainment. I ask myself, could anyone standing face to face with people who actually do suffer violence and sexual exploitation "explain" that these tragedies, portrayed in virtual form, are considered merely "entertainment"?

There is also something sinister which stems from the fact that freedom and tolerance are so often separated from truth. This is fuelled by the notion, widely held today, that there are no absolute truths to guide our lives. Relativism, by indiscriminately giving value to practically everything, has made "experience" all-important. Yet, experiences, detached from any consideration of what is good or true, can lead, not to genuine freedom, but to moral or intellectual confusion, to a lowering of standards, to a loss of self-respect, and even to despair.

Dear friends, life is not governed by chance; it is not random. Your very existence has been willed by God, blessed and given a purpose (cf. *Gen* 1:28)! Life is not just a succession of events or experiences, helpful though many of them are. It is a search for the true, the good and the beautiful. It is to this end that we make our choices; it is for this that we exercise our freedom; it is in this – in truth, in goodness, and in beauty – that we find happiness and joy. Do not be fooled by those who see you as just another consumer in a market of undifferentiated possibilities, where choice itself becomes the good, novelty usurps beauty, and subjective experience displaces truth.

Christ offers more! Indeed he offers everything! Only he who is the Truth can be the Way and hence also the Life. Thus the "way" which the Apostles brought to the ends of the earth is life in Christ. This is the life of the Church.

And the entrance to this life, to the Christian way, is Baptism.

This evening I wish therefore to recall briefly something of our understanding of Baptism before tomorrow considering the Holy Spirit. On the day of your Baptism, God drew you into his holiness (cf. *2 Pet* 1:4). You were adopted as a son or daughter of the Father. You were incorporated into Christ. You were made a dwelling place of his Spirit (cf. *1 Cor* 6:19). Indeed, towards the conclusion of your Baptism, the priest turned to your parents and those gathered and, calling you by your name, said: "you have become a new creation" (*Rite of Baptism*, 99).

Dear friends, in your homes, schools and universities, in your places of work and recreation, remember that you are a new creation! As Christians you stand in this world knowing that God has a human face – Jesus Christ – the "way" who satisfies all human yearning, and the "life" to which we are called to bear witness, walking always in his light (cf. *ibid.*, 100).

The task of witness is not easy. There are many today who claim that God should be left on the sidelines, and that religion and faith, while fine for individuals, should either be excluded from the public forum altogether or included only in the pursuit of limited pragmatic goals. This secularist vision seeks to explain human life and shape society with little or no reference to the Creator. It presents itself as neutral, impartial and inclusive of everyone. But in reality, like every ideology, secularism imposes a world-view. If God is irrelevant to public life, then society will be shaped in a godless image. When God is eclipsed, our ability to recognize the natural order, purpose, and the "good" begins to wane. What was ostensibly promoted as human ingenuity soon manifests itself as folly, greed and selfish exploitation. And so we have become more and more aware of our need for humility before the delicate complexity of God's world.

But what of our social environment? Are we equally alert to the signs of turning our back on the moral structure with which God has endowed humanity (cf. *2007 World Day of Peace Message*, 8)? Do we recognize that the innate dignity of every individual rests on his or her deepest identity – as image of the Creator – and therefore that human rights are universal, based on the natural law, and not something dependent upon negotiation or patronage, let alone compromise? And so we are led to reflect on what place the poor and the elderly, immigrants and the voiceless, have in our societies. How can it be that domestic violence torments so many mothers and children? How can it be that the most wondrous and sacred human space – the womb – has become a place of unutterable violence?

My dear friends, God's creation is one and it is good. The concerns for non-violence, sustainable development, justice and peace, and care for our environment are of vital importance for humanity. They cannot, however, be understood apart from a profound reflection upon the innate dignity of every human life from conception to natural death: a dignity conferred by God himself and thus inviolable. Our world has grown weary of greed, exploitation and division, of the tedium of false idols and piecemeal responses, and the pain of false promises. Our hearts and minds are yearning for a vision of life where love endures, where gifts are shared, where unity is built, where freedom finds meaning in truth, and where identity is found in respectful communion. This is the work of the Holy Spirit! This is the hope held out by the Gospel of Jesus Christ. It is to bear witness to this reality that you were created anew at Baptism and strengthened through the gifts of the Spirit at Confirmation. Let this be the message that you bring from Sydney to the world!

Greetings in Various Languages

[Italian] *Mi rivolgo ora con affetto ai giovani di lingua italiana. Cari amici, anche questa volta avete risposto numerosi al mio invito, nonostante le difficoltà dovute alla distanza. Vi ringrazio, e voglio salutare anche i vostri coetanei che dall'Italia sono spiritualmente uniti a noi. Vi invito a vivere con grande impegno interiore queste giornate: aprite il cuore al dono dello Spirito Santo, per essere rafforzati nella fede e nella capacità di rendere testimonianza al Signore risorto. Arrivederci!*

[French] *Chers jeunes francophones, poussés par le désir d'approfondir votre foi, vous êtes venus des extrémités de la terre pour vivre à Sydney l'expérience unique et communautaire d'une rencontre privilégiée avec le Seigneur. C'est l'Esprit Saint qui vous a rassemblés ici. Puisse-t-Il vous permettre de expérimenter sa présence dans votre cœur et vous pousser à rendre témoignage avec ardeur de Jésus-Christ mort et ressuscité pour vous!*

[German] *Liebe Freunde, die ihr mich in meiner Muttersprache versteht, von Herzen grüße ich euch alle. Erweist euch überall als freudige Zeugen der frohmachenden Botschaft Jesu! Sprecht mutig von eurem Glauben, auch wenn ihr zuweilen auf Widerspruch stößt und das Kreuz der Ablehnung erfährt. Der Herr, der für uns ein größeres Kreuz getragen hat, wird euch beistehen. Gott schenke euch eine gute, gesegnete Zeit hier in Australien.*

[Spanish] *Queridos jóvenes de lengua española, la misión de ser testigos del Señor en todos los lugares de la tierra es una apasionante tarea, que exige acoger su Palabra e identificarse con Él, compartiendo con los demás la alegría de haber encontrado al verdadero amigo que nunca defrauda. Que este reto agrande vuestra generosidad. Un saludo muy cordial a todos.*

[Portuguese] *Queridos amigos dos vários países de língua oficial portuguesa, bem-vindos a Sidney! A todos saúdo com afecto: os de perto e os de longe. Lá, na vossa Pátria, tereis ouvido Jesus segredar-vos: «Sereis minhas testemunhas… até aos confins do mundo»* (Acts *1, 8). A viagem mais ou menos longa que enfrentastes para chegar até aqui, à Austrália ou – de seu nome cristão completo – «Terra Austral do Espírito Santo», não deixou em vós a sensação de terdes chegado aos confins do mundo? Pois bem! É com grande alegria que o Papa vos acolhe para vos confirmar como testemunhas de Jesus, por Ele acreditadas com o dom do seu próprio Espírito.*

3

Ecumenical Meeting

Crypt of St. Mary's Cathedral, Sydney
Friday, 18 July 2008

Dear Brothers and Sisters in Christ,

I give heartfelt thanks to God for this opportunity to meet and pray with all of you who have come here representing various Christian communities in Australia. Grateful for Bishop Forsyth's and Cardinal Pell's words of welcome, I joyfully greet you in the name of the Lord Jesus, the "cornerstone" of the "household of God" (*Eph* 2:19-20). I would like to offer a particular greeting to Cardinal Edward Cassidy, former President of the Pontifical Council for Promoting Christian Unity, who, due to ill health, could not be with us today. I recall with gratitude his steadfast dedication to improving mutual understanding among all Christians, and I would ask all of you to join me in praying for his speedy recovery.

Australia is a country marked by much ethnic and religious diversity. Immigrants arrive on the shores of this majestic land hoping to find happiness and opportunities for employment. Yours, too, is a nation which recognizes the importance of religious freedom. This is a fundamental right which, when respected, allows citizens to act upon values which are rooted in their deepest beliefs, contributing thus to the well-being of society. In this way, Christians cooperate, together with members of other religions, for the promotion of human dignity and for fellowship among all nations.

Australians cherish cordial and frank discussion. This has served the ecumenical movement well. An example would be the *Covenant* signed in 2004 by the members of the National Council of Churches in Australia. This document recognizes a common commitment, sets out goals, and acknowledges points of convergence without glossing over differences. Such an approach demonstrates not only the possibility of formulating concrete resolutions for fruitful cooperation in the present day, but also the need to continue patient discussion on theological points of difference. May your ongoing deliberations in the Council of Churches and in other local forums be sustained by what you have already achieved.

This year we celebrate the two thousandth anniversary of the birth of Saint Paul, a tireless worker for unity in the early Church. In the scripture passage we have just heard, Paul reminds us of the tremendous grace we have received in becoming members of Christ's body through baptism. This sacrament, the entryway to the Church and the "bond of unity" for everyone reborn through it (cf. *Unitatis Redintegratio*, 22), is accordingly the point of departure for the entire ecumenical movement. Yet it is not the final destination. The road of ecumenism ultimately points towards a common celebration of the Eucharist (cf. *Ut Unum Sint*, 23-24; 45), which Christ entrusted to his Apostles as the sacrament of the Church's unity *par excellence*. Although there are still obstacles to be overcome, we can be sure that a common Eucharist one day would only strengthen our resolve to love and serve one another in imitation of our Lord: for Jesus' commandment to "do this in memory of me" (*Lk* 22:19) is intrinsically ordered to his admonition to "wash one another's feet" (*Jn* 13:14). For this reason, a candid dialogue concerning the place of the Eucharist – stimulated by a renewed and attentive study of scripture, patristic writings, and documents from across the two millennia of Christian history (cf. *Ut Unum Sint*, 69-70) – will undoubtedly help to advance the ecumenical movement and unify our witness to the world.

Dear friends in Christ, I think you would agree that the ecumenical movement has reached a critical juncture. To move forward, we must continually ask God to renew our minds with the Holy Spirit (cf. *Rom* 12:2), who speaks to us through the scriptures and guides us into all truth (cf. 2 *Pet* 1:20-21; *Jn* 16:13). We must guard against any temptation to view doctrine as divisive and hence an impediment to the seemingly more pressing and immediate task of improving the world in which we live. In fact, the history of the Church demonstrates that *praxis* is not only inseparable from, but actually flows out of *didache* or teaching. The more closely we strive for a deeper understanding of the divine mysteries, the more eloquently our works of charity will speak of God's bountiful goodness and love towards all. Saint Augustine expressed the nexus between the gift of understanding and the virtue of charity when he wrote that the mind returns to God by love (cf. *De Moribus Ecclesiae Catholicae*, XII, 21), and that wherever one sees charity, one sees the Trinity (*De Trinitate*, 8, 8, 12).

For this reason, ecumenical dialogue advances not only through an exchange of ideas but by a sharing in mutually enriching gifts (cf. *Ut Unum Sint*, 28; 57). An "idea" aims at truth; a "gift" expresses love. Both are essential to dialogue. Opening ourselves to accept spiritual gifts from other Christians quickens our ability to perceive the light of truth which comes from the Holy Spirit. Saint Paul teaches that it is within the *koinonia* of the Church that we have access to and the means of safeguarding the truth of the Gospel, for the Church is "built upon the foundation of the apostles and prophets" with Jesus himself as the cornerstone (*Eph* 2:20).

In this light, perhaps we might consider the complementary biblical images of "body" and "temple" used to describe the Church. By employing the image of a body (cf. *1 Cor* 12:12-31), Paul draws attention to the organic unity and diversity that allows the Church to breathe and grow. Equally significant, however, is the image of a solid, well-structured temple composed of living stones rising on its sure foundation. Jesus himself brings together in perfect unity these images of "temple" and "body" (cf. *Jn* 2:21-22; *Lk* 23:45; *Rev* 21:22).

Every element of the Church's structure is important, yet all of them would falter and crumble without the cornerstone who is Christ. As "fellow citizens" of the "household of God", Christians must work together to ensure that the edifice stands strong so that others will be attracted to enter and discover the abundant treasures of grace within. As we promote Christian values, we must not neglect to proclaim their source by giving a common witness to Jesus Christ the Lord. It is he who commissioned the apostles, he whom the prophets preached, and he whom we offer to the world.

Dear friends, your presence fills me with the ardent hope that as we pursue together the path to full unity, we will have the courage to give common witness to Christ. Paul speaks of the importance of the prophets in the early Church; we too have received a prophetic calling through our baptism. I am confident that the Spirit will open our eyes to see the gifts of others, our hearts to receive his power, and our minds to perceive the light of Christ's truth. I express heartfelt thanks to all of you for the time, scholarship and talent which you have invested for the sake of the "one body and one spirit" (*Eph* 4:4; cf. *1 Cor* 12:13) which the Lord willed for his people and for which he gave his very life. All glory and power be to him for ever and ever. Amen!

Pilgrims carry the World Youth Day cross through the streets of Sydney, before gathering around it for prayer in Hyde Park.

Left: The World Youth Day icon is installed at Barangaroo, East Darling Harbour.

Below: Cardinal George Pell, the Archbishop of the host city, Sydney, greets a very young pilgrim and her family at the Opening Mass.

Pope Benedict travels to the Welcoming Ceremony at Barangaroo by 'Boatmobile' where he is greeted by an estimated 200,000 people from more than 170 countries.

World Youth Day is a prayerful encounter for the young, and for the young at heart.

4

Meeting with Representatives of Other Religions

Chapter Hall of St. Mary's Cathedral, Sydney
Friday, 18 July 2008

Dear Friends,

I extend cordial greetings of peace and goodwill to all of you who are here representing various religious traditions in Australia. Grateful for this encounter, I thank Rabbi Jeremy Lawrence and Sheikh Mohamadu Saleem for the words of welcome which they expressed in their own name and on behalf of your respective communities.

Australia is renowned for the congeniality of its people towards neighbour and visitor alike. It is a nation that holds freedom of religion in high regard. Your country recognizes that a respect for this fundamental right gives men and women the latitude to worship God according to their conscience, to nurture their spirits, and to act upon the ethical convictions that stem from their beliefs.

A harmonious relationship between religion and public life is all the more important at a time when some people have come to consider religion as a cause of division rather than a force for unity. In a world threatened by sinister and indiscriminate forms of violence, the unified voice of religious people urges nations and communities to resolve conflicts through peaceful means and with full regard for human dignity. One of the many ways religion stands at the service of mankind is by offering a vision of the human person that highlights our innate aspiration to live generously, forging bonds of friendship with our neighbours. At their core, human relations cannot be defined in terms of power, domination and self-interest. Rather, they reflect and perfect man's natural inclination to live in communion and accord with others.

The religious sense planted within the human heart opens men and women to God and leads them to discover that personal fulfilment does not consist in the selfish gratification of ephemeral desires. Rather, it leads us to meet the needs of others and to search for concrete ways to contribute to the common good. Religions have a special role in this regard, for they teach people that authentic service requires sacrifice and self-discipline, which in turn must be cultivated through self-denial, temperance and a moderate use of the world's goods. In this way, men and women are led to regard the environment as a marvel to be pondered and respected rather than a commodity for mere consumption. It is incumbent upon religious people to demonstrate that it is possible to find joy in living simply and modestly, generously sharing one's surplus with those suffering from want.

Friends, these values, I am sure you will agree, are particularly important to the adequate formation of young people, who are so often tempted to view life itself as a commodity. They also have an aptitude for self-mastery: indeed, in sports, the creative arts, and in academic studies, they readily welcome it as a challenge. Is it not true that when presented with high ideals, many young people are attracted to asceticism and the practice of moral virtue through self-respect and a concern for others? They delight in contemplating the gift of creation and are intrigued by the mystery of the transcendent. In this regard, both faith schools and State schools could do even more to nurture the spiritual dimension of every young person. In Australia, as elsewhere, religion has been a motivating factor in the foundation of many educational institutions, and rightly it continues to occupy a place in school curricula today. The theme of education frequently emerges from the deliberations of the Interfaith Cooperation for Peace and Harmony, and I warmly encourage those participating in this initiative to continue the conversation about the values that integrate the intellectual, human and religious dimensions of a sound education.

The world's religions draw constant attention to the wonder of human existence. Who can help but marvel at the power of the mind to grasp the secrets of nature through scientific discovery? Who is not stirred by the possibility of forming a vision for the future? Who is not impressed by the power of the human spirit to set goals and to develop ways of achieving them? Men and women are endowed with the ability not only to imagine how things might be better, but to invest their energies to make them better. We are conscious of our unique relationship to the natural realm. If, then, we believe that we are not subject to the laws of the material universe in the same way as the rest of creation, should we not make goodness, compassion, freedom, solidarity, and respect for every individual an essential part of our vision for a more humane future?

Yet religion, by reminding us of human finitude and weakness, also enjoins us not to place our ultimate hope in this passing world. Man is "like a breath, his days are like a passing shadow" (*Ps* 144:4). All of us have experienced the disappointment of falling short of the good we wish to accomplish and the difficulty of making the right choice in complex situations.

The Church shares these observations with other religions. Motivated by charity, she approaches dialogue believing that the true source of freedom is found in the person of Jesus of Nazareth. Christians believe it is he who fully discloses the human potential for virtue and goodness, and he who liberates us from sin and darkness. The universality of human experience, which transcends all geographical boundaries and cultural limitations, makes it possible for followers of religions to engage in dialogue so as to grapple with the mystery of life's joys and sufferings. In this regard, the Church eagerly seeks opportunities to listen to the spiritual experience of other religions. We could say that all religions aim to penetrate the profound meaning of human existence by linking it to an origin or principle outside itself. Religions offer an attempt to understand the cosmos as coming from and returning to this origin or principle. Christians believe that God has revealed this origin and principle in Jesus, whom the Bible refers to as the "Alpha and Omega" (cf. *Rev* 1:8; 22:1).

My dear friends, I have come to Australia as an ambassador of peace. For this reason, I feel blessed to meet you who likewise share this yearning and the desire to help the world attain it. Our quest for peace goes hand in hand with our search for meaning, for it is in discovering the truth that we find the sure road to peace (cf. *Message for World Day of Peace*, 2006). Our effort to bring about reconciliation between peoples springs from, and is directed to, that truth which gives purpose to life. Religion offers peace, but more importantly, it arouses within the human spirit a thirst for truth and a hunger for virtue. May we encourage everyone – especially the young – to marvel at the beauty of life, to seek its ultimate meaning, and to strive to realize its sublime potential!

With these sentiments of respect and encouragement, I commend you to the providence of Almighty God, and I assure you of my prayers for you and your loved ones, the members of your communities, and all the citizens of Australia.

5

Meeting with a Group of Disadvantaged Young People

of the Rehabilitation Community of the University of Notre Dame

Church of the Sacred Heart, Darlinghurst (Sydney)
Friday, 18 July 2008

Dear Young Friends,

I am pleased to be with you at Darlinghurst today, and I warmly greet all those taking part in the "Alive" programme, as well as the staff who run it. I pray that you will all benefit from the assistance offered by the Archdiocese of Sydney's Social Services Agency, and that the good work being done here will continue long into the future.

The name of the programme you are following prompts us to ask the question: what does it really mean to be "alive", to live life to the full? This is what all of us want, especially when we are young, and it is what Christ wants for us. In fact, he said: "I have come that they may have life, and have it abundantly" (*Jn* 10:10). The most basic instinct of all living things is to stay alive, to grow, to flourish, and to pass on the gift of life to others. So it is only natural that we should ask how best to do this.

For the people of the Old Testament, this question was just as urgent as it is for us today. No doubt they listened attentively when Moses said to them: "I set before you life or death, blessing or curse. Choose life, then, so that you and your descendants may live in the love of the Lord your God, obeying his voice, clinging to him – for in this your life consists" (*Dt* 30:19-20). It was clear what they had to do: they had to turn away from other gods and worship the true God who had revealed himself to Moses – and they had to obey his commandments. You might think that in today's world, people are unlikely to start worshipping other gods. But sometimes people worship "other gods" without realizing it. False "gods", whatever name, shape or form we give them, are nearly always associated with the worship of three things: material possessions, possessive love, or power. Let me explain what I mean.

Material possessions, in themselves, are good. We would not survive for long without money, clothing and shelter. We must eat in order to stay alive. Yet if we are greedy, if we refuse to share what we have with the hungry and the poor, then we make our possessions into a false god. How many voices in our materialist society tell us that happiness is to be found by acquiring as many possessions and luxuries as we can! But this is to make possessions into a false god. Instead of bringing life, they bring death.

Authentic love is obviously something good. Without it, life would hardly be worth living. It fulfils our deepest need, and when we love, we become most fully ourselves, most fully human. But how easily it can be made into a false god! People often think they are being loving when actually they are being possessive or manipulative. People sometimes treat others as objects to satisfy their own needs rather than as persons to be loved and cherished. How easy it is to be deceived by the many voices in our society that advocate a permissive approach to sexuality, without regard for modesty, self-respect or the moral values that bring quality to human relationships! This is worship of a false god. Instead of bringing life, it brings death.

The power God has given us to shape the world around us is obviously something good. Used properly and responsibly, it enables us to transform people's lives. Every community needs good leaders. Yet how tempting it can be to grasp at power for its own sake, to seek to dominate others or to exploit the natural environment for selfish purposes! This is to make power into a false god. Instead of bringing life, it brings death.

The cult of material possessions, the cult of possessive love and the cult of power often lead people to attempt to "play God": to try to seize total control, with no regard for the wisdom or the commandments that God has made known to us. This is the path that leads towards death. By contrast, worship of the one true God means recognizing in him the source of all goodness, entrusting ourselves to him, opening ourselves to the healing power of his grace and obeying his commandments: that is the way to choose life.

A vivid illustration of what it means to turn back from the path of death onto the path of life is found in a Gospel story that I am sure you all know well: the parable of the prodigal son. When that young man left his father's house at the beginning of the story, he was seeking the illusory pleasures promised by false "gods". He squandered his inheritance on a life of indulgence, and ended up in abject poverty and misery. When he reached the very lowest point, hungry and abandoned, he realized how foolish he had been to leave his loving father. Humbly, he returned and asked forgiveness. Joyfully his father embraced him and exclaimed: "This son of mine was dead, and has come back to life; he was lost, and is found" (*Lk* 15:24).

Many of you must have had personal experience of what that young man went through. Perhaps you have made choices that you now regret, choices that led you down a path which, however attractive it appeared at the time, only led you deeper into misery and abandonment. The choice to abuse drugs or alcohol, to engage in criminal activity or self-harm, may have seemed at the time to offer a way out of a difficult or confusing situation. You now know that, instead of bringing life, it brings death. I wish to acknowledge your courage in choosing to turn back onto the path of life, just like the young man in the parable. You have accepted help – from friends or family, from the staff who run the "Alive" programme: from people who care deeply for your well-being and happiness.

Dear friends, I see you as ambassadors of hope to others in similar situations. You can convince them of the need to choose the path of life and shun the path of death, because you speak from experience. All through the Gospels, it was those who had taken wrong turnings who were particularly loved by Jesus, because once they recognized their mistake, they were all the more open to his healing message. Indeed, Jesus was often criticized by self-righteous members of society for spending so much time with such people. "Why does your master eat with tax collectors and sinners?", they asked. He responded: "It is not the healthy who need the doctor, but the sick … I did not come to call the virtuous but sinners" (cf. *Mt* 9:11-13). It was those who were willing to rebuild their lives who were most ready to listen to Jesus and become his disciples. You can follow in their footsteps, you too can grow particularly close to Jesus because you have chosen to turn back towards him. You can be sure that, just like the Father in the story of the prodigal son, Jesus welcomes you with open arms. He offers you unconditional love – and it is in loving friendship with him that the fullness of life is to be found.

I mentioned earlier that when we love we are fulfilling our deepest need and becoming most fully ourselves, most fully human. Loving is what we are programmed to do, what we were designed for by our Creator. Naturally, I am not talking about fleeting, shallow relationships, I am talking about real love, the very heart of Jesus' moral teaching: "You must love the Lord your God with all your heart, with all your soul, with all your mind, and with all your strength" and "You must love your neighbour as yourself" (cf. *Mk* 12:30-31). This, if you like, is the programme that is hard-wired into every human person, if only we had the wisdom and generosity to live by it, if only we were ready to sacrifice our own preferences so as to be of service to others, to give our lives for the good of others, and above all for Jesus, who loved us and gave his life for us. That is what human beings are called to do, that is what it means to be truly alive.

Dear young friends, my message to you today is the same one that Moses proposed all those years ago. "Choose life, so that you and your descendants may live in the love of the Lord your God". Let his Spirit guide you onto the path of life, so that you obey his commandments, follow his teachings, leave behind the wrong turnings that lead only to death, and commit yourselves to a lifelong friendship with Jesus Christ. In the power of the Holy Spirit, choose life and choose love, and bear witness before the world to the joy that it brings. That is my prayer for each one of you this World Youth Day. May God bless you all.

6

Eucharistic Celebration with Bishops, Seminarians and Novices

Saint Mary's Cathedral, Sydney
Saturday, 19 July 2008

Dear Brothers and Sisters,

In this noble cathedral I rejoice to greet my brother Bishops and priests, and the deacons, religious and laity of the Archdiocese of Sydney. In a very special way, my greeting goes to the seminarians and young religious who are present among us. Like the young Israelites in today's first reading, they are a sign of hope and renewal for God's people; and, like those young Israelites, they will have the task of building up the Lord's house in the coming generation. As we admire this magnificent edifice, how can we not think of all those ranks of priests, religious and faithful laity who, each in his or her own way, contributed to the building up of the Church in Australia? Our thoughts turn in particular to those settler families to whom Father Jeremiah O'Flynn entrusted the Blessed Sacrament at his departure, a "small flock" which cherished and preserved that precious treasure, passing it on to the succeeding generations who raised this great tabernacle to the glory of God. Let us rejoice in their fidelity and perseverance, and dedicate ourselves to carrying on their labours for the spread of the Gospel, the conversion of hearts and the growth of the Church in holiness, unity and charity!

We are about to celebrate the dedication of the new altar of this venerable cathedral. As its sculpted frontal powerfully reminds us, every altar is a symbol of Jesus Christ, present in the midst of his Church as priest, altar and victim (cf. *Preface of Easter* V). Crucified, buried and raised from the dead, given life in the Spirit and seated at the right hand of the Father, Christ has become our great high priest, eternally making intercession for us. In the Church's liturgy, and above all in the sacrifice of the Mass consummated on the altars of the world, he invites us, the members of his mystical Body, to share in his self-oblation. He calls us, as the priestly people of the new and eternal covenant, to offer, in union with him, our own daily sacrifices for the salvation of the world.

In today's liturgy the Church reminds us that, like this altar, we too have been consecrated, set "apart" for the service of God and the building up of his Kingdom. All too often, however, we find ourselves immersed in a world that would set God "aside". In the name of human freedom and autonomy, God's name is passed over in silence, religion is reduced to private devotion, and faith is shunned in the public square. At times this mentality, so completely at odds with the core of the Gospel, can even cloud our own understanding of the Church and her mission. We too can be tempted to make the life of faith a matter of mere sentiment, thus blunting its power to inspire a consistent vision of the world and a rigorous dialogue with the many other visions competing for the minds and hearts of our contemporaries.

Yet history, including the history of our own time, shows that the question of God will never be silenced, and that indifference to the religious dimension of human existence ultimately diminishes and betrays man himself. Is that not the message which is proclaimed by the magnificent architecture of this cathedral? Is that not the mystery of faith which will be proclaimed from this altar at every celebration of the Eucharist? Faith teaches us that in Jesus Christ, the incarnate Word, we come to understand the grandeur of our own humanity, the mystery of our life on this earth, and the sublime destiny which awaits us in heaven (cf. *Gaudium et Spes*, 24). Faith teaches us that we are God's creatures, made in his image and likeness, endowed with an inviolable dignity, and called to eternal life. Wherever man is diminished, the world around us is also diminished; it loses its ultimate meaning and strays from its goal. What emerges is a culture, not of life, but of death. How could this be considered "progress"? It is a backward step, a form of regression which ultimately dries up the very sources of life for individuals and all of society.

We know that in the end – as Saint Ignatius of Loyola saw so clearly – the only real "standard" against which all human reality can be measured is the Cross and its message of an unmerited love which triumphs over evil, sin and death, creating new life and unfading joy. The Cross reveals that we find ourselves only by giving our lives away, receiving God's love as an unmerited gift and working to draw all men and women into the beauty of that love and the light of the truth which alone brings salvation to the world.

It is in this truth – this mystery of faith – that we have been "consecrated" (cf. *Jn* 17:17-19), and it is in this truth that we are called to grow, with the help of God's grace, in daily fidelity to his word, within the life-giving communion of the Church. Yet how difficult is this path of consecration! It demands continual "conversion", a sacrificial death to self which is the condition for belonging fully to God, a change of mind and heart which brings true freedom and a new breadth of vision. Today's liturgy offers an eloquent symbol of that progressive spiritual transformation to which each of us is called. From the sprinkling of water, the proclamation of God's word and the invocation of all the saints, to the prayer of consecration, the anointing and washing of the altar, its being clothed in white and apparelled in light – all these rites invite us to re-live our own consecration in Baptism. They invite us to reject sin and its false allure, and to drink ever more deeply from the life-giving springs of God's grace.

Dear friends, may this celebration, in the presence of the Successor of Peter, be a moment of rededication and renewal for the whole Church in Australia! Here I would like to pause to acknowledge the shame which we have all felt as a result of the sexual abuse of minors by some clergy and religious in this country. Indeed, I am deeply sorry for the pain and suffering the victims have endured, and I assure them that, as their Pastor, I too share in their suffering. These misdeeds, which constitute so grave a betrayal of trust, deserve unequivocal condemnation. They have caused great pain and have damaged the Church's witness. I ask all of you to support and assist your Bishops, and to work together with them in combating this evil. Victims should receive compassion and care, and those responsible for these evils must be brought to justice. It is an urgent priority to promote a safer and more wholesome environment, especially for young people. In these days marked by the celebration of World Youth Day, we are reminded of how precious a treasure has been entrusted to us in our young people, and how great a part of the Church's mission in this country has been dedicated to their education and care. As the Church in Australia continues, in the spirit of the Gospel, to address effectively this serious pastoral challenge, I join you in praying that this time of purification will bring about healing, reconciliation and ever greater fidelity to the moral demands of the Gospel.

I wish now to turn to the seminarians and young religious in our midst, with a special word of affection and encouragement. Dear friends: with great generosity you have set out on a particular path of consecration, grounded in your Baptism and undertaken in response to the Lord's personal call. You have committed yourselves, in different ways, to accepting Christ's invitation to follow him, to leave all behind, and to devote your lives to the pursuit of holiness and the service of his people.

In today's Gospel, the Lord calls us to "believe in the light" (*Jn* 12:36). These words have a special meaning for you, dear young seminarians and religious. They are a summons to trust in the truth of God's word and to hope firmly in his promises. They invite us to see, with the eyes of faith, the infallible working of his grace all around us, even in those dark times when all our efforts seem to be in vain. Let this altar, with its powerful image of Christ the Suffering Servant, be a constant inspiration to you. Certainly there are times when every faithful disciple will feel the heat and the burden of the day (cf. *Mt* 20:12), and the struggle of bearing prophetic witness before a world which can appear deaf to the demands of God's word. Do not be afraid! Believe in the light! Take to heart the truth which we have heard in today's second reading: "Jesus Christ is the same, yesterday, today and for ever" (*Heb* 13:8). The light of Easter continues to dispel the darkness!

The Lord also calls us to walk in the light (cf. *Jn* 12:35). Each of you has embarked on the greatest and the most glorious of all struggles, to be consecrated in truth, to grow in virtue, to achieve harmony between your thoughts and ideals, and your words and actions. Enter sincerely and deeply into the discipline and spirit of your programmes of formation. Walk in Christ's light daily through fidelity to personal and liturgical prayer, nourished by meditation on the inspired word of God. The Fathers of the Church loved to see the Scriptures as a spiritual Eden, a garden where we can walk freely with God, admiring the beauty and harmony of his saving plan as it bears fruit in our own lives, in the life of the Church and in all of history. Let prayer, then, and meditation on God's word, be the lamp which illumines, purifies and guides your steps along the path which the Lord has marked out for you. Make the daily celebration of the Eucharist the centre of your life. At each Mass, when the Lord's Body and

Blood are lifted up at the end of the Eucharistic Prayer, lift up your own hearts and lives, through Christ, with him and in him, in the unity of the Holy Spirit, as a loving sacrifice to God our Father.

In this way, dear young seminarians and religious, you yourselves will become living altars, where Christ's sacrificial love is made present as an inspiration and a source of spiritual nourishment to everyone you meet. By embracing the Lord's call to follow him in chastity, poverty and obedience, you have begun a journey of radical discipleship which will make you "signs of contradiction" (cf. *Lk* 2:34) to many of your contemporaries. Model your lives daily on the Lord's own loving self-oblation in obedience to the will of the Father. You will then discover the freedom and joy which can draw others to the Love which lies beyond all other loves as their source and their ultimate fulfilment. Never forget that celibacy for the sake of the Kingdom means embracing a life completely devoted to love, a love that enables you to commit yourselves fully to God's service and to be totally present to your brothers and sisters, especially those in need. The greatest treasures that you share with other young people – your idealism, your generosity, your time and energy – these are the very sacrifices which you are placing upon the Lord's altar. May you always cherish this beautiful charism which God has given you for his glory and the building up of the Church!

Dear friends, let me conclude these reflections by drawing your attention to the great stained glass window in the chancel of this cathedral. There Our Lady, Queen of Heaven, is represented enthroned in majesty beside her divine Son. The artist has represented Mary, as the new Eve, offering an apple to Christ, the new Adam. This gesture symbolizes her reversal of our first parents' disobedience, the rich fruit which God's grace bore in her own life, and the first fruits of that redeemed and glorified humanity which she has preceded into the glory of heaven. Let us ask Mary, Help of Christians, to sustain the Church in Australia in fidelity to that grace by which the Crucified Lord even now "draws to himself" all creation and every human heart (cf. *Jn* 12:32). May the power of his Holy Spirit consecrate the faithful of this land in truth, and bring forth abundant fruits of holiness and justice for the redemption of the world. May it guide all humanity into the fullness of life around that Altar, where, in the glory of the heavenly liturgy, we are called to sing God's praises for ever. Amen.

7

Vigil with the Young People

Randwick Racecourse
Saturday, 19 July 2008

Dear Young People,

Once again this evening we have heard Christ's great promise – "you will receive power when the Holy Spirit has come upon you". And we have heard his summons – "be my witnesses throughout the world" – (*Acts* 1:8). These were the very last words which Jesus spoke before his Ascension into heaven. How the Apostles felt upon hearing them, we can only imagine. But we do know that their deep love for Jesus, and their trust in his word, prompted them to gather and to wait; to wait not aimlessly, but together, united in prayer, with the women and Mary in the Upper Room (cf. *Acts* 1:14). Tonight, we do the same. Gathered before our much-travelled Cross and the icon of Mary, and under the magnificent constellation of the Southern Cross, we pray. Tonight, I am praying for you and for young people throughout the world. Be inspired by the example of your Patrons! Accept into your hearts and minds the sevenfold gift of the Holy Spirit! Recognize and believe in the power of the Spirit in your lives!

The other day we talked of the unity and harmony of God's creation and our place within it. We recalled how in the great gift of baptism we, who are made in God's image and likeness, have been reborn, we have become God's adopted children, a new creation. And so it is as children of Christ's light – symbolized by the lit candles you now hold – that we bear witness in our world to the radiance no darkness can overcome (cf. *Jn* 1:5).

Tonight we focus our attention on *how* to become witnesses. We need to understand the person of the Holy Spirit and his vivifying presence in our lives. This is not easy to comprehend. Indeed the variety of images found in scripture referring to the Spirit – wind, fire, breath – indicate our struggle to articulate an understanding of him. Yet we do know that it is the Holy Spirit who, though silent and unseen, gives direction and definition to our witness to Jesus Christ.

You are already well aware that our Christian witness is offered to a world which in many ways is fragile. The unity of God's creation is weakened by wounds which run particularly deep when social relations break apart, or when the human spirit is all but crushed through the exploitation and abuse of persons. Indeed, society today is being fragmented by a way of thinking that is inherently short-sighted, because it disregards the full horizon of truth – the truth about God and about us. By its nature, relativism fails to see the whole picture. It ignores the very principles which enable us to live and flourish in unity, order and harmony.

What is our response, as Christian witnesses, to a divided and fragmented world? How can we offer the hope of peace, healing and harmony to those "stations" of conflict, suffering, and tension through which you have chosen to march with this World Youth Day Cross? Unity and reconciliation cannot be achieved through our efforts alone. God has made us for one another (cf. *Gen* 2:24) and only in God and his Church can we find the unity we seek. Yet, in the face of imperfections and disappointments – both individual and institutional – we are sometimes tempted to construct artificially a "perfect" community. That temptation is not new. The history of the Church includes many examples of attempts to bypass or override human weaknesses or failures in order to create a perfect unity, a spiritual utopia.

Such attempts to construct unity in fact undermine it! To separate the Holy Spirit from Christ present in the Church's institutional structure would compromise the unity of the Christian community, which is precisely the Spirit's gift! It would betray the nature of the Church as the living temple of the Holy Spirit (cf. *1 Cor* 3:16). It is the Spirit, in fact, who guides the Church in the way of all truth and unifies her in communion and in the works of ministry (cf. *Lumen Gentium*, 4). Unfortunately the temptation to "go it alone" persists. Some today portray their local community as somehow separate from the so-called institutional Church, by speaking of the former as flexible and open to the Spirit and the latter as rigid and devoid of the Spirit.

Unity is of the essence of the Church (cf. *Catechism of the Catholic Church*, 813); it is a gift we must recognize and cherish. Tonight, let us pray for the resolve to nurture unity: contribute to it! resist any temptation to walk away!

For it is precisely the comprehensiveness, the vast vision, of our faith – solid yet open, consistent yet dynamic, true yet constantly growing in insight – that we can offer our world. Dear young people, is it not because of your faith that friends in difficulty or seeking meaning in their lives have turned to you? Be watchful! Listen! Through the dissonance and division of our world, can you hear the concordant voice of humanity? From the forlorn child in a Darfur camp, or a troubled teenager, or an anxious parent in any suburb, or perhaps even now from the depth of your own heart, there emerges the same human cry for recognition, for belonging, for unity. Who satisfies that essential human yearning to be one, to be immersed in communion, to be built up, to be led to truth? The Holy Spirit! This is the Spirit's role: to bring Christ's work to fulfilment. Enriched with the Spirit's gifts, you will have the power to move beyond the piecemeal, the hollow utopia, the fleeting, to offer the consistency and certainty of Christian witness!

Friends, when reciting the Creed we state: "We believe in the Holy Spirit, the Lord, the giver of life". The "Creator Spirit" is the power of God giving life to all creation and the source of new and abundant life in Christ. The Spirit sustains the Church in union with the Lord and in fidelity to the apostolic Tradition. He inspired the Sacred Scriptures and he guides God's People into the fullness of truth (cf. *Jn* 16:13) In all these ways the Spirit is the "giver of life", leading us into the very heart of God. So, the more we allow the Spirit to direct us, the more perfect will be our configuration to Christ and the deeper our immersion in the life of the Triune God.

This sharing in God's nature (cf. 2 *Pet* 1:4) occurs in the unfolding of the everyday moments of our lives where he is always present (cf. *Bar* 3:38). There are times, however, when we might be tempted to seek a certain fulfilment apart from God. Jesus himself asked the Twelve: "do you also wish to go away?" Such drifting away perhaps offers the illusion of freedom. But where does it lead? To whom would we go? For in our hearts we know that it is the Lord who has "the words of eternal life" (*Jn* 6:67-68). To turn away from him is only a futile attempt to escape from ourselves (cf. Saint Augustine, *Confessions* VIII, 7). God is with us in the reality of life, not the fantasy! It is embrace, not escape, that we seek! So the Holy Spirit gently but surely steers us back to what is real, what is lasting, what is true. It is the Spirit who leads us back into the communion of the Blessed Trinity!

The Holy Spirit has been in some ways the neglected person of the Blessed Trinity. A clear understanding of the Spirit almost seems beyond our reach. Yet, when I was a small boy, my parents, like yours, taught me the Sign of the Cross. So, I soon came to realize that there is one God in three Persons, and that the Trinity is the centre of our Christian faith and life. While I grew up to have some understanding of God the Father and the Son – the names already conveyed much – my understanding of the third person of the Trinity remained incomplete. So, as a young priest teaching theology, I decided to study the outstanding witnesses to the Spirit in the Church's history. It was on this journey that I found myself reading, among others, the great Saint Augustine.

Augustine's understanding of the Holy Spirit evolved gradually; it was a struggle. As a young man he had followed Manichaeism – one of those attempts I mentioned earlier, to create a spiritual utopia by radically separating the things of the spirit from the things of the flesh. Hence he was at first suspicious of the Christian teaching that God had become man. Yet his experience of the love of God present in the Church led him to investigate its source in the life of the Triune God. This led him to three particular insights about the Holy Spirit as the bond of unity within the Blessed Trinity: unity as communion, unity as abiding love, and unity as giving and gift. These three insights are not just theoretical. They help explain how the Spirit works. In a world where both individuals and communities often suffer from an absence of unity or cohesion, these insights help us remain attuned to the Spirit and to extend and clarify the scope of our witness.

So, with Augustine's help, let us illustrate something of the Holy Spirit's work. He noted that the two words "Holy" and "Spirit" refer to what is divine about God; in other words what is shared by the Father and the Son – their *communion*. So, if the distinguishing characteristic of the Holy Spirit is to be what is *shared* by the Father and the Son, Augustine concluded that the Spirit's particular quality is *unity*. It is a unity of lived communion: a unity of persons in a relationship of constant giving, the Father and the Son giving themselves to each other. We begin to glimpse, I think, how illuminating is this understanding of the Holy Spirit as unity, as communion. True unity could never be founded upon relationships which deny the equal dignity of other persons. Nor is unity simply the sum total of the groups through which we sometimes attempt to "define" ourselves. In fact, only in the life of communion is unity sustained and human identity fulfilled: we recognize the common need for God, we respond to the unifying presence of the Holy Spirit, and we give ourselves to one another in service.

Augustine's second insight – the Holy Spirit as abiding love – comes from his study of the First Letter of Saint John. John tells us that "God is love" (*1 Jn* 4:16). Augustine suggests that while these words refer to the Trinity as a whole they express a particular characteristic of the Holy Spirit. Reflecting on the lasting nature of love – "whoever abides in love remains in God and God in him" (*ibid.*) – he wondered: is it love or the Holy Spirit which grants the abiding? This is the conclusion he reaches: "The Holy Spirit makes us remain in God and God in us; yet it is love that effects this. The Spirit therefore is God as love!" (*De Trinitate,* 15.17.31). It is a beautiful explanation: God shares himself as love in the Holy Spirit. What further understanding might we gain from this insight? Love is the sign of the presence of the Holy Spirit! Ideas or voices which lack love – even if they seem sophisticated or knowledgeable – cannot be "of the Spirit". Furthermore, love has a particular trait: far from being indulgent or fickle, it has a task or purpose to fulfil: to abide. By its nature love is enduring. Again, dear friends, we catch a further glimpse of how much the Holy Spirit offers our world: love which dispels uncertainty; love which overcomes the fear of betrayal; love which carries eternity within; the true love which draws us into a unity that abides!

The third insight – the Holy Spirit as gift – Augustine derived from meditating on a Gospel passage we all know and love: Christ's conversation with the Samaritan woman at the well. Here Jesus reveals himself as the giver of the living water (cf. *Jn* 4:10) which later is explained as the Holy Spirit (cf. *Jn* 7:39; *1 Cor* 12:13). The Spirit is "God's gift" (*Jn* 4:10) – the internal spring (cf. *Jn* 4:14), who truly satisfies our deepest thirst and leads us to the Father. From this observation Augustine concludes that God sharing himself with us as gift is the Holy Spirit (cf. *De Trinitate*, 15, 18, 32). Friends, again we catch a glimpse of the Trinity at work: the Holy Spirit is God eternally giving himself; like a never-ending spring he pours forth nothing less than himself. In view of this ceaseless gift, we come to see the limitations of all that perishes, the folly of the consumerist mindset. We begin to understand why the quest for novelty leaves us unsatisfied and wanting. Are we not looking for an eternal gift? The spring that will never run dry? With the Samaritan woman, let us exclaim: give me this water that I may thirst no more! (cf. *Jn* 4:15).

Dear young people, we have seen that it is the Holy Spirit who brings about the wonderful communion of believers in Jesus Christ. True to his nature as giver and gift alike, he is even now working through you. Inspired by the insights of Saint Augustine: let *unifying love* be your measure; *abiding love* your challenge; *self-giving love* your mission!

Tomorrow, that same gift of the Spirit will be solemnly

conferred upon our confirmation candidates. I shall pray: "give them the spirit of wisdom and understanding, the spirit of right judgement and courage, the spirit of knowledge and reverence … and fill them with the spirit of wonder and awe". These gifts of the Spirit – each of which, as Saint Francis de Sales reminds us, is a way to participate in the one love of God – are neither prizes nor rewards. They are freely given (cf. *1 Cor* 12:11). And they require only one response on the part of the receiver: I accept! Here we sense something of the deep mystery of being Christian. What constitutes our faith is not primarily what we do but what we receive. After all, many generous people who are not Christian may well achieve far more than we do. Friends, do you accept being drawn into God's Trinitarian life? Do you accept being drawn into his communion of love?

The Spirit's gifts working within us give direction and definition to our witness. Directed to unity, the gifts of the Spirit bind us more closely to the whole Body of Christ (cf. *Lumen Gentium*, 11), equipping us better to build up the Church in order to serve the world (cf. *Eph* 4:13). They call us to active and joyful participation in the life of the Church: in parishes and ecclesial movements, in religious education classes, in university chaplaincies and other catholic organizations. Yes, the Church must grow in unity, must be strengthened in holiness, must be rejuvenated, must be constantly renewed (cf. *Lumen Gentium*, 4). But according to whose standard? The Holy Spirit's! Turn to him, dear young people, and you will find the true meaning of renewal.

Tonight, gathered under the beauty of the night sky, our hearts and minds are filled with gratitude to God for the great gift of our Trinitarian faith. We recall our parents and grandparents who walked alongside us when we, as children, were taking our first steps in our pilgrim journey of faith. Now many years later, you have gathered as young adults with the Successor of Peter. I am filled with deep joy to be with you. Let us invoke the Holy Spirit: he is the artisan of God's works (cf. *Catechism of the Catholic Church*, 741). Let his gifts shape you! Just as the Church travels the same journey with all humanity, so too you are called to exercise the Spirit's gifts amidst the ups and downs of your daily life. Let your faith mature through your studies, work, sport, music and art. Let it be sustained by prayer and nurtured by the sacraments, and thus be a source of inspiration and help to those around you. In the end, life is not about accumulation. It is much more than success. To be truly alive is to be transformed from within, open to the energy of God's love. In accepting the power of the Holy Spirit you too can transform your families, communities and nations. Set free the gifts! Let wisdom, courage, awe and reverence be the marks of greatness!

Greetings in Various Languages

[Italian] *Cari giovani italiani! Un saluto speciale a tutti voi! Custodite la fiamma che lo Spirito Santo ha acceso nei vostri cuori, perché non abbia a spegnersi, ma anzi arda sempre più e diffonda luce e calore a chi incontrerete sulla vostra strada, specialmente a quanti hanno smarrito la fede e la speranza. La Vergine Maria vegli su di voi in questa notte ed ogni giorno della vostra vita.*

[French] *Chers jeunes de langue française, vous êtes venus prier ce soir l'Esprit-Saint. Sa présence silencieuse en votre cœur vous fera comprendre peu à peu le dessein de Dieu sur vous. Puisse-t-Il vous accompagner dans votre vie quotidienne et vous conduire vers une meilleure connaissance de Dieu et de votre prochain! C'est Lui qui du plus profond de votre être vous pousse vers l'unique Vérité divine et vous fait vivre authentiquement en frères.*

[German] *Einen frohen Gruß richte ich an euch, liebe junge Christen aus den Ländern deutscher Sprache. Der Heilige Geist, der Botschafter der göttlichen Liebe, will in euren Herzen wohnen. Gebt ihm Raum in euch im Hören auf Gottes Wort, im Gebet und in eurer Solidarität mit den Armen und Leidenden. Bringt den Geist des Friedens und der Versöhnung zu den Menschen. Gott, von dem alles Gute kommt, vollende jedes gute Werk, das ihr zu seiner Ehre tut.*

[Spanish] *Queridos amigos, el Espíritu Santo dirige nuestros pasos para seguir a Jesucristo en el mundo de hoy, que espera de los cristianos una palabra de aliento y un testimonio de vida que inviten a mirar confiadamente hacia el futuro. Os encomiendo en mis plegarias, para que respondáis generosamente a lo que el Señor os pide y a lo que todos los hombres anhelan. Que Dios os bendiga.*

[Portuguese] *Meus queridos amigos, recebei o Espírito Santo, para serdes Igreja! Igreja quer dizer todos nós unidos como um corpo que recebe o seu influxo vital de Jesus ressuscitado. Este dom é maior que os nossos corações, porque brota das entranhas da Santíssima Trindade. Fruto e condição: sentir-se parte uns dos outros, viver em comunhão. Para isso, jovens caríssimos, acolhei dentro de vós a força de vida que há em Jesus. Deixai-O entrar no vosso coração. Deixai-vos plasmar pelo Espírito Santo.*

And now, as we move towards adoration of the Blessed Sacrament, in stillness and expectation, I echo to you the words spoken by Blessed Mary MacKillop when she was just twenty-six years old: "Believe in the whisperings of God to your heart!" Believe in him! Believe in the power of the Spirit of Love!

From vantage points around the city, giant screens enable pilgrims to follow the Way of the Cross.

Pope Benedict holds a lighted candle during the Saturday evening Vigil at Randwick racecourse. An indigenous woman carries a torch lit by the Holy Father. In turn, she will light the torches of twelve pilgrims.

At the evening Vigil, Pope Benedict gives the blessing during Benediction to pilgrims holding lighted candles.

Pope Benedict prepares to enter the sanctuary for the World Youth Day Mass at Randwick racecourse. The canopy over the sanctuary is adorned by a painting of a dove, representing the Holy Spirit, by Marjorie Liddy from the Tiwi Islands. An estimated 400,000 pilgrims participated in the Mass.

Pope Benedict greets the pilgrims at the World Youth Day Mass.

Young pilgrims from Spain rejoice in the choice of Madrid, as the host city for the World Youth Day to be held in 2011.

8

Eucharistic Celebration on the Occasion of the 23rd World Youth Day

Randwick Racecourse
Sunday, 20 July 2008

Dear Friends,

"You will receive power when the Holy Spirit comes upon you" (*Acts* 1:8). We have seen this promise fulfilled! On the day of Pentecost, as we heard in the first reading, the Risen Lord, seated at the right hand of the Father, sent the Spirit upon the disciples gathered in the Upper Room. In the power of that Spirit, Peter and the Apostles went forth to preach the Gospel to the ends of the earth. In every age, and in every language, the Church throughout the world continues to proclaim the marvels of God and to call all nations and peoples to faith, hope and new life in Christ.

In these days I too have come, as the Successor of Saint Peter, to this magnificent land of Australia. I have come to confirm you, my young brothers and sisters, in your faith and to encourage you to open your hearts to the power of Christ's Spirit and the richness of his gifts. I pray that this great assembly, which unites young people "from every nation under heaven" (cf. *Acts* 2:5), will be a new Upper

Room. May the fire of God's love descend to fill your hearts, unite you ever more fully to the Lord and his Church, and send you forth, a new generation of apostles, to bring the world to Christ!

"You will receive power when the Holy Spirit comes upon you". These words of the Risen Lord have a special meaning for those young people who will be confirmed, sealed with the gift of the Holy Spirit, at today's Mass. But they are also addressed to each of us – to all those who have received the Spirit's gift of reconciliation and new life at Baptism, who have welcomed him into their hearts as their helper and guide at Confirmation, and who daily grow in his gifts of grace through the Holy Eucharist. At each Mass, in fact, the Holy Spirit descends anew, invoked by the solemn prayer of the Church, not only to transform our gifts of bread and wine into the Lord's body and blood, but also to transform our lives, to make us, in his power, "one body, one spirit in Christ".

But what is this "power" of the Holy Spirit? It is the power of God's life! It is the power of the same Spirit who hovered over the waters at the dawn of creation and who, in the fullness of time, raised Jesus from the dead. It is the power which points us, and our world, towards the coming of the Kingdom of God. In today's Gospel, Jesus proclaims that a new age has begun, in which the Holy Spirit will be poured out upon all humanity (cf. *Lk* 4:21). He himself, conceived by the Holy Spirit and born of the Virgin May, came among us to bring us that Spirit. As the source of our new life in Christ, the Holy Spirit is also, in a very real way, the soul of the Church, the love which binds us to the Lord and one another, and the light which opens our eyes to see all around us the wonders of God's grace.

Here in Australia, this "great south land of the Holy Spirit", all of us have had an unforgettable experience of the Spirit's presence and power in the beauty of nature. Our eyes have been opened to see the world around us as it truly is: "charged", as the poet says, "with the grandeur of God", filled with the glory of his creative love. Here too, in this great assembly of young Christians from all over the world, we have had a vivid experience of the Spirit's presence and power in the life of the Church. We have seen the Church for what she truly is: the Body of Christ, a living community of love, embracing people of every race, nation and tongue, of every time and place, in the unity born of our faith in the Risen Lord.

The power of the Spirit never ceases to fill the Church with life! Through the grace of the Church's sacraments, that power also flows deep within us, like an underground river which nourishes our spirit and draws us ever nearer to the source of our true life, which is Christ. Saint Ignatius of Antioch, who died a martyr in Rome at the beginning of the second century, has left us a splendid description of the Spirit's power dwelling within us. He spoke of the Spirit as a fountain of living water springing up within his heart and whispering: "Come, come to the Father" (cf. *Ad Rom.*, 6:1-9).

Yet this power, the grace of the Spirit, is not something we can merit or achieve, but only receive as pure gift. God's love can only unleash its power when it is allowed to change us from within. We have to let it break through the hard crust of our indifference, our spiritual weariness, our blind conformity to the spirit of this age. Only then can we let it ignite our imagination and shape our deepest desires. That is why prayer is so important: daily prayer, private prayer in the quiet of our hearts and before the Blessed Sacrament, and liturgical prayer in the heart of the Church. Prayer is pure receptivity to God's grace, love in action, communion with the Spirit who dwells within us, leading us, through Jesus, in the Church, to our heavenly Father. In the power of his Spirit, Jesus is always present in our hearts, quietly waiting for us to be still with him, to hear his voice, to abide in his love, and to receive "power from on high", enabling us to be salt and light for our world.

At his Ascension, the Risen Lord told his disciples: "You will be my witnesses … to the ends of the earth" (*Acts* 1:8). Here, in Australia, let us thank the Lord for the gift of faith, which has come down to us like a treasure passed on from generation to generation in the communion of the Church. Here, in Oceania, let us give thanks in a special way for all those heroic missionaries, dedicated priests and religious, Christian parents and grandparents, teachers and catechists who built up the Church in these lands – witnesses like Blessed Mary MacKillop, Saint Peter Chanel, Blessed Peter To Rot, and so many others! The power of the Spirit, revealed in their lives, is still at work in the good they left behind, in the society which they shaped and which is being handed on to you.

Dear young people, let me now ask you a question. What will *you* leave to the next generation? Are you building your lives on firm foundations, building something that will endure? Are you living your lives in a way that opens up space for the Spirit in the midst of a world that wants to forget God, or even rejects him in the name of a falsely-conceived freedom? How are you using the gifts you have been given, the "power" which the Holy Spirit is even now prepared to release within you? What legacy will you leave to young people yet to come? What difference will you make?

The power of the Holy Spirit does not only enlighten and console us. It also points us to the future, to the coming of God's Kingdom. What a magnificent vision of a humanity redeemed and renewed we see in the new age promised by today's Gospel! Saint Luke tells us that Jesus Christ is the fulfilment of all God's promises, the Messiah who fully possesses the Holy Spirit in order to bestow that gift upon all mankind. The outpouring of Christ's Spirit upon humanity is a pledge of hope and deliverance from everything that impoverishes us. It gives the blind new sight; it sets the downtrodden free, and it creates unity in and through diversity (cf. *Lk* 4:18-19; *Is* 61:1-2). This power can create a new world: it can "renew the face of the earth" (cf. *Ps* 104:30)!

Empowered by the Spirit, and drawing upon faith's rich vision, a new generation of Christians is being called to help build a world in which God's gift of life is welcomed, respected and cherished – not rejected, feared as a threat and destroyed. A new age in which love is not greedy or self-seeking, but pure, faithful and genuinely free, open to others, respectful of their dignity, seeking their good, radiating joy and beauty. A new age in which hope liberates us from the shallowness, apathy and self-absorption which deaden our souls and poison our relationships. Dear young friends, the Lord is asking you to be prophets of this new age, messengers of his love, drawing people to the Father and building a future of hope for all humanity.

The world needs this renewal! In so many of our societies, side by side with material prosperity, a spiritual desert is spreading: an interior emptiness, an unnamed fear, a quiet sense of despair. How many of our contemporaries have built broken and empty cisterns (cf. *Jer* 2:13) in a desperate search for meaning – the ultimate meaning that only love can give? This is the great and liberating gift which the Gospel brings: it reveals our dignity as men and women created in the image and likeness of God. It reveals humanity's sublime calling, which is to find fulfilment in love. It discloses the truth about man and the truth about life.

The Church also needs this renewal! She needs your faith, your idealism and your generosity, so that she can always be young in the Spirit (cf. *Lumen Gentium*, 4)! In today's second reading, the Apostle Paul reminds us that each and every Christian has received a gift meant for building up the Body of Christ. The Church especially needs the gifts of young people, all young people. She needs to grow in the power of the Spirit who even now gives joy to your youth and inspires you to serve the Lord with gladness. Open your hearts to that power! I address this plea in a special way to those of you whom the Lord is calling to the priesthood and the consecrated life. Do not be afraid to say "yes" to Jesus, to find your joy in doing his will, giving yourself completely to the pursuit of holiness, and using all your talents in the service of others!

In a few moments, we will celebrate the sacrament of Confirmation. The Holy Spirit will descend upon the confirmands; they will be "sealed" with the gift of the Spirit and sent forth to be Christ's witnesses. What does it mean to receive the "seal" of the Holy Spirit? It means being indelibly marked, inalterably changed, a new creation. For those who have received this gift, nothing can ever be the same! Being "baptized" in the one Spirit (cf. *1 Cor* 12:13) means being set on fire with the love of God. Being "given to drink" of the Spirit means being refreshed by the beauty of the Lord's plan for us and for the world, and becoming in turn a source of spiritual refreshment for others. Being "sealed with the Spirit" means not being afraid to stand up for Christ, letting the truth of the Gospel permeate the way we see, think and act, as we work for the triumph of the civilization of love.

As we pray for the confirmands, let us ask that the power of the Holy Spirit will revive the grace of our own Confirmation. May he pour out his gifts in abundance on all present, on this city of Sydney, on this land of Australia and on all its people! May each of us be renewed in the spirit of wisdom and understanding, the spirit of right judgement and courage, the spirit of knowledge and reverence, the spirit of wonder and awe in God's presence!

Through the loving intercession of Mary, Mother of the Church, may this Twenty-third World Youth Day be experienced as a new Upper Room, from which all of us, burning with the fire and love of the Holy Spirit, go forth to proclaim the Risen Christ and to draw every heart to him! Amen.

Greetings in Various Languages

[Italian] *Saluto di cuore i giovani di lingua italiana, ed estendo il mio affettuoso pensiero a quanti sono originari dell'Italia e vivono in Australia. Al termine di questa straordinaria esperienza di Chiesa, che ci ha fatto vivere una rinnovata Pentecoste, tornate a casa rinvigoriti dalla forza dello Spirito Santo. Siate testimoni di Cristo risorto, speranza dei giovani e dell'intera famiglia umana!*

[French] *Chers jeunes francophones, l'Esprit Saint est la source du message de Jésus-Christ et de son action salvifique. Il parle au cœur de chacun le langage qu'il comprend. La diversité des dons de l'Esprit vous fait comprendre la richesse de grâces qui est en Dieu. Puissiez-vous vous ouvrir à son souffle ! Puissiez-vous permettre son action en vous et autour de vous ! Vous vivrez ainsi en Dieu et vous témoignerez que le Christ est le Sauveur que le monde espère.*

[German] *Auch euch, liebe junge Freunde deutscher Sprache, gilt mein herzlicher Gruß. Der Heilige Geist ist ein Geist der Gemeinschaft und wirkt Verständigung und Kommunikation. Sprecht mit anderen über eure Hoffnungen und Ideale, und sprecht von Gott und mit Gott! Glücklich ist der Mensch, der in der Liebe Gottes und in der Liebe zum Nächsten lebt. Gottes Geist führe euch auf Wegen des Friedens!*

[Spanish] *Queridos jóvenes, en Cristo se cumplen todas las promesas de salvación verdadera para la humanidad. Él tiene para cada uno de vosotros un proyecto de amor en el que se encuentra el sentido y la plenitud de la vida, y espera de todos vosotros que hagáis fructificar los dones que os ha dado, siendo sus testigos de palabra y con el propio ejemplo. No lo defraudéis.*

[Portuguese] *Amados jovens de língua portuguesa, queridos amigos em Cristo! Sabeis que Jesus não vos quer sozinhos; disse Ele: «Eu rogarei ao Pai e Ele vos dará outro Consolador para estar convosco para sempre, o Espírito da verdade (...) que vós conheceis, porque habita convosco e está em vós» (Jo 14, 16-17). É verdade! Sobre vós desceu uma língua de fogo do Pentecostes: é a vossa marca de cristãos. Mas não foi para a guardardes só para vós, porque «a manifestação do Espírito é dada a cada um para proveito comum» (1 Cor 12, 7). Levai este Fogo santo a todos os cantos da terra. Nada e ninguém O poderá apagar, porque desceu do céu. Tal é a vossa força, caros jovens amigos! Por isso, vivei do Espírito e para o Espírito!*

9

Angelus Message

Randwick Racecourse
Sunday, 20 July 2008

Dear Friends,

In the beautiful prayer that we are about to recite, we reflect on Mary as a young woman, receiving the Lord's summons to dedicate her life to him in a very particular way, a way that would involve the generous gift of herself, her womanhood, her motherhood. Imagine how she must have felt. She was filled with apprehension, utterly overwhelmed at the prospect that lay before her.

The angel understood her anxiety and immediately sought to reassure her. "Do not be afraid, Mary … The Holy Spirit will come upon you and the power of the Most High will overshadow you" (*Lk* 1: 30, 35). It was the Spirit who gave her the strength and courage to respond to the Lord's call. It was the Spirit who helped her to understand the great mystery that was to be accomplished through her. It was the Spirit who enfolded her with his love and enabled her to conceive the Son of God in her womb.

This scene is perhaps the pivotal moment in God's relationship with his people. God revealed himself partially, gradually, as we all do in our personal relationships. It took time for the chosen people to develop their relationship with God. The covenant with Israel was like a period of courtship, a long engagement. Then came the definitive moment, the moment of marriage, the establishment of a new and everlasting covenant. As Mary stood before the Lord, she represented the whole of humanity. In the angel's message, it was as if God made a marriage proposal to the human race. And in our name, Mary said "yes".

In fairy tales, the story ends there, and all "live happily ever after". In real life it is not so simple. For Mary there were many struggles ahead, as she lived out the consequences of the "yes" that she had given to the Lord. Simeon prophesied that a sword would pierce her heart. When Jesus was twelve years old, she experienced every parent's worst nightmare when, for three days, the child went missing. And after his public ministry, she suffered the agony of witnessing to his crucifixion and death. Throughout her trials she remained faithful to her promise, sustained by the Spirit of fortitude. And she was gloriously rewarded.

Dear young people, we too must remain faithful to the "yes" that we have given to the Lord's offer of friendship. We know that he will never abandon us. We know that he will always sustain us through the gifts of the Spirit. Mary accepted the Lord's "proposal" in our name. So let us turn to her and ask her to guide us as we struggle to remain faithful to the life-giving relationship that God has established with each one of us. She is our example and our inspiration, she intercedes for us with her Son, and with a mother's love she shields us from harm.

Post Angelus

The time has come for me to say goodbye – or rather, to say *arrivaderci*! I thank you all for participating in World Youth Day, here in Sydney, and I look forward to seeing you again in three years' time. World Youth Day 2011 will take place in Madrid, Spain. Until then, let us continue to pray for one another, and let us joyfully bear witness to Christ before the world. May God bless you all.

10

To volunteers of the 23rd World Youth Day

Domain, Sydney
Monday, 21 July 2008

Dear Friends in Christ,

I thank Bishop Fisher and Cardinal Pell for their words and I am pleased to have this opportunity to bid farewell to all of you and to say what a wonderful experience this week has been. During these days we have been able to witness at first hand the joy that so many thousands of young people find in their faith, and we have been able to offer praise and thanksgiving to God for his goodness to us. We have had a taste of the warmth and generosity of Australian hospitality, and we have glimpsed something of the glorious scenery of this beautiful continent. It has truly been a week to remember.

None of this would have been possible, though, without a great deal of preparation and sheer hard work during the period leading up to World Youth Day. I want to thank all of you for the generous commitment of time and energy you have made, in order to ensure the smooth running of each of the events we have celebrated together. They have all required careful coordination, involving civil authorities, police and first aid agencies, as well as church personnel and a vast array of volunteers, marshals and stewards. Your efforts have prepared the ground for the Spirit to come down in power, forging bonds of unity and friendship among young people from widely differing backgrounds, and rekindling their love for Jesus Christ and his Church. In the crowds that have assembled here in Sydney we have seen a vivid expression of the unity-in-diversity of the universal Church, a vision in microcosm of the united human family that we long to see. In the power of the Spirit, may these young people make that vision a reality in the world of tomorrow.

I shall have an opportunity at the airport to thank the representatives of the civil authorities. Here I want to express my deep gratitude to all the bishops, priests, men and women religious, chaplains, teachers, lay associations, ecclesial movements, host families, schools and parish communities who have given so much to make World Youth Day a success. I thank particularly Bishop Anthony Fisher and Mr Danny Casey, who have worked so hard to coordinate all the different activities. We read in the Acts of the Apostles that "it is more blessed to give than to receive" (20:35) – but I trust that you will nevertheless have received much from those you have served so generously in the course of our celebrations. To all of you, I say a sincere and heartfelt "thank you".

As I set off on my journey back to Rome, I shall treasure the memory of the many grace-filled events we have experienced together: from my first encounter with the young people at Barangaroo, through the meetings at Darlinghurst and Saint Mary's Cathedral, to the Youth Vigil at Southern Cross

Precinct and the Final Mass there yesterday. I pray that you too will take many precious memories and spiritual insights away with you, and will return to your homes and families with fresh zeal to spread the Gospel of Jesus Christ. In the power of the Spirit, go forth now to renew the face of the earth!

As I bid you a fond farewell, I commend all of you to the loving intercession of Our Lady of the Southern Cross, Help of Christians, I invoke upon you the sevenfold gifts of the Holy Spirit, and I assure you of my continued prayers. God bless the young people of our world and God bless the people of Australia!

11

Farewell Ceremony

International Airport of Sydney
Monday, 21 July 2008

Dear Friends,

Before I take my leave, I wish to say to my hosts how much I have enjoyed my visit here and how grateful I am for your hospitality. I thank the Prime Minister, the Honourable Kevin Rudd, for the kindness he has shown to me and to all the participants at World Youth Day. I also thank the Governor-General, Major-General Michael Jeffery, for his presence here and for graciously receiving me at Admiralty House at the start of my public engagements. The Federal Government and the State Government of New South Wales, as well as the residents and the business community of Sydney, have been most cooperative in their support of World Youth Day. An event of this kind requires an immense amount of preparation and organization, and I know that I speak on behalf of many thousands of young people when I express my appreciation and gratitude to you all. In characteristic Australian style, you have extended a warm welcome to me and to countless young pilgrims who have flocked here from every corner of the globe. To the host families in Australia and New Zealand who have made room for the young people in their homes, I am especially grateful. You have opened your doors and your hearts to the world's youth, and on their behalf I thank you.

The principal actors on the stage over these last few days, of course, have been the young people themselves. World Youth Day is their day. It is they who have made this a global ecclesial event, a great celebration of youth and a great celebration of what it is to be the Church, the people of God throughout the world, united in faith and love and empowered by the Spirit to bear witness to the risen Christ to the ends of the earth. I thank them for coming, I thank them for their participation, and I pray that they will have a safe journey home. I know that the young people, their families and their sponsors have in many cases made great sacrifices to enable them to travel to Australia. For this the entire Church is grateful.

As I look back over these stirring days, there are many scenes that stand out in my mind. I was deeply moved by my visit to the Mary MacKillop Memorial, and I thank the Sisters of Saint Joseph for the opportunity to pray at the Shrine of their Co-Foundress. The Stations of the Cross in the streets of Sydney were a powerful reminder that Christ loved us "to the end" and shared our sufferings so that we could share his glory. The meeting with the young people at Darlinghurst was a moment of joy and great hope, a sign that Christ can lift us out of the most difficult situations, restoring our dignity and enabling us to look forward to a brighter future. The meeting with ecumenical and interreligious leaders was marked by a spirit of genuine fraternity and a deep desire for greater collaboration in building a more just and peaceful world. And without doubt, the gatherings at Barangaroo and Southern Cross were high-points of my visit. Those experiences of prayer, and our joyful celebration of the Eucharist, were an eloquent testimony to the life-giving work of the Holy Spirit, present and active in the hearts of our young people. World Youth Day has shown us that the Church can rejoice in the young people of today and be filled with hope for the world of tomorrow.

Dear friends, as I depart from Sydney, I ask God to look down lovingly upon this city, this country and all its inhabitants. I pray that many of their number will be inspired by Blessed Mary MacKillop's example of compassion and service. And as I bid you farewell with deep gratitude in my heart, I say once again: May God bless the people of Australia!

Appendix

Homily for the World Youth Day Opening Mass

By + Cardinal George Pell
Archbishop of Sydney

Barangaroo, Sydney Harbour
Tuesday, 15 July 2008

We all know that Christ Our Lord is often described as the Good Shepherd of today's responsorial psalm (*Ps* 23). We are told that he leads us near restful waters, revives our flagging spirits, enables us to rest peacefully.

In developing this image on one occasion, Jesus explained that such a shepherd was prepared to leave the ninety-nine sheep to search out the one who was lost.

Few countries today have a shepherd who cares for only twenty or thirty sheep, and in Australia with large farms and huge flocks Our Lord's advice is not very practical. If the lost sheep was valuable and probably healthy, it might make sense to take the time to search for it. More usually it would be left behind or its absence not even noticed.

Jesus was saying that both he and his Father are not like this, because he knows each one of his sheep and like a good father he goes searching for the lost one he loves, particularly if it is sick, or in trouble, or unable to help itself.

Earlier in this Mass I welcomed you all to this World Youth Day week and I repeat that welcome now. But I do not begin with the ninety-nine healthy sheep, those of you already open to the Spirit, perhaps already steady witnesses to faith and love. I begin by welcoming and encouraging anyone, anywhere who regards himself or herself as lost, in deep distress, with hope diminished or even exhausted.

Young or old, woman or man, Christ is still calling those who are suffering to come to him for healing, as he has for two thousand years. The causes of the wounds are quite secondary, whether they be drugs or alcohol, family breakups, the lusts of the flesh, loneliness or a death. Perhaps even the emptiness of success.

Christ's call is to all who are suffering, not just to Catholics or other Christians, but especially to those without religion. Christ is calling you home; to love, healing and community.

Our first reading today (*Ezek* 37:1-14) was from Ezekiel who, with Isaiah and Jeremiah, was one of the three greatest Jewish prophets. Many parts of Australia are still in drought, so all Australians understand a valley of dry bones and fleshless skeletons. But this grim vision is offered first of all to any and all of you who are even tempted to say "our hope is gone, we are as good as dead".

This is never true while we can still choose. While there is life there is always the option of hope and with Christian hope come faith and love. Until the end we are always able to choose and act.

This vision of the valley of the dry bones, the most spectacular in the whole of the Bible, was given when the hand of God came upon Ezekiel while the Jews were in captivity in Babylon, probably earlier rather than later in the sixth century B.C. For about 150 years the political fortunes of the Jewish people had been in decline, first of all at the hands of the Assyrians. Later in 587 B.C. came the final catastrophic defeat and their transportation into exile. The Jewish people were in despair, powerless to change their situation.

This is the historical background to Ezekiel's dramatic vision where the dead were well dead, whitened skeletons as the birds of prey had long finished their ghastly business of stripping off the flesh. It was an immense battlefield of the unburied.

A hesitant and reluctant Ezekiel was urged by God to prophesy to these bones and as he did so the bones rushed together noisily, accompanied by an earthquake. Sinews knitted them together, flesh and then skin clothed the corpses.

Another stage was needed and the breath, or Spirit, came from the four corners of the earth as the bodies came "to life again and stood up on their feet, a great and immense army".

We see this vision as a prefiguration of the resurrection of the dead, the Jews of Ezekiel's time did not believe in such a conception of the afterlife. For them the immense resurrected army represented all the Jewish people, those from the northern kingdom taken off to Assyria, those at home and those in Babylon. They were to be reconstituted as a people in their own land and they would know that the one true God alone had done this. And all this came to pass.

Over the centuries we Christians have used this passage liturgically at Easter, especially for the baptism of catechumens on Holy Saturday night and it is, of course, a powerful image of the one true God's regenerative power for this life and eternity.

Secular wisdom claims that leopards do not change their spots, but we Christians believe in the power of the Spirit to convert and change persons away from evil to good; from fear and uncertainty to faith and hope.

Believers are heartened by Ezekiel's vision, because we know the power of God's forgiveness, the capacity of Christ and the Catholic tradition to cause new life to flourish even in unlikely circumstances.

That same power glimpsed in Ezekiel's vision is offered to us today, to all of us without exception. You young pilgrims can look ahead to the future stretching out before you, so rich in promise. The Gospel parable of the sower and the seed (*Lk* 8:4-15) reminds you of the great opportunity you have to embrace your vocation and produce an abundant harvest, a hundredfold crop.

Matthew, Mark and Luke all place this story of the sower at the beginning of their collection of Jesus' parables. It explains some fundamental truths about the challenges of Christian discipleship and lists the alternatives to a fruitful Christian life. Fidelity is not automatic or inevitable.

One detail makes the parable more plausible, because it seems the Jews in Our Lord's time threw the seed on the ground before they ploughed it, so explaining a little better the seed being in unlikely places rather than just in the furrows.

Are we amongst those whose faith has already been snatched away by the devil, as Our Lord explained the image of the birds of the sky gobbling up the seed? No one at this Mass would be in that category. Some might be like the seed on rocky ground which could not put down roots. Those here in this second category are likely to be striving to start again in the spiritual life, or at least examining the possibility of doing so. But most of us are in the third and fourth categories, where the seed has fallen on good soil and is growing and flourishing; or we are in danger of being choked off by the worries of life. All of us, including those who are no longer young, have to pray for wisdom and perseverance.

I have no problem in believing that Our Lord spelt out the meaning of this parable to his closest followers and that he would have been asked by them regularly to do so. But the disciples' enquiries provoked a disconcerting response, when Our Lord divides his listeners into two groups: those to whom the mysteries of the Kingdom are revealed and the rest for whom the parables remain only parables. This second group is described in words from the prophet Isaiah as those who "may see but not perceive, listen but not understand". Probably the background to this is the amazement of Our Lord's disciples at the large number who did not accept his teaching.

Why is this still so? What must we do to be among those for whom the mysteries of the Kingdom are revealed?

The call of the one true God remains mysterious, especially today when many good people find it hard to believe. Even in the time of the prophets many of their hearers remained spiritually deaf and blind, while any number over the ages have admired the beauty of Jesus' teaching, but never been moved to answer his call.

Our task is to be open to the power of the Spirit, to allow the God of surprises to act through us. Human motivation is complex and mysterious, because sometimes very strong Catholics, and other strong Christians, can be prayerful and regularly good, but also very determined not to take even one further step. On the other hand, some followers of Christ can be much less zealous and faithful, but open to development, to change for the better because they realize their unworthiness and their ignorance. Where do you stand?

Whatever our situation we must pray for an openness of heart, for a willingness to take the next step, even if we are fearful of venturing too much further. If we take God's hand, he will do the rest. Trust is the key. God will not fail us.

How can we work to avoid slipping from the last and best category of the fruit bearers into those "who are choked by the worries and riches and pleasures of life" and so do not produce much fruit at all?

The second reading from Paul's letter to the Galatians (5:16-17, 22-25) points us in the correct direction, reminding us all that each person must declare himself in the age-old struggle between good and evil, between what Paul calls the flesh and the Spirit. It is not good enough to be only a passenger, to try to live in "no-mans land" between the warring parties. Life forces us to choose, eventually destroys any possibility of neutrality.

We will bring forth good fruit by learning the language of the Cross and inscribing it on our hearts. The language of the Cross brings us the fruits of the Spirit which Paul lists, enables us to experience peace and joy, to be regularly kind and generous to others. Following Christ is not cost free, not always easy, because it requires struggling against what St. Paul calls "the flesh", our fat relentless egos, old fashioned selfishness. It is always a battle, even for old people like me!

Don't spend your life sitting on the fence, keeping your options open, because only commitments bring fulfilment. Happiness comes from meeting our obligations, doing our duty, especially in small matters and regularly, so we can rise to meet the harder challenges. Many have found their life's calling at World Youth Days.

To be a disciple of Jesus requires discipline, especially self-discipline; what Paul calls self-control. The practice of self-control won't make you perfect (it hasn't with me), but self-control is necessary to develop and protect the love in our hearts and prevent others, especially our family and friends, from being hurt by our lapses into nastiness or laziness.

I pray that through the power of the Spirit all of you will join that immense army of saints, healed and reborn, which was revealed to Ezekiel, which has enriched human history for countless generations and which is rewarded in the afterlife of heaven.

Let me conclude by adapting one of the most powerful sermons of St. Augustine, the finest theologian of the first millennium and a bishop in the small North African town of Hippo around 1600 years ago.

During the next five days of prayer and celebration I expect that that your spirits will rise, as mine always does, in the excitement of World Youth Day. Please God we shall all be glad that we participated, despite the cost, hassles and distances travelled. During this week we have every right to rejoice and celebrate the liberation of our repentance, the rejuvenation of our faith. We are called to open our hearts to the power of the Spirit. And to the young ones I give a gentle reminder that in your enthusiasm and excitement you do not forget to listen and pray!

Many of you have travelled such a long way that you may believe that you have arrived, indeed, at the ends of earth! If so, that's good, for Our Lord told his first apostles that they would be his witnesses in Jerusalem and to the ends of the earth. That prophecy has been fulfilled in the witness of many missionaries to this vast southern continent, and it is fulfilled yet again in your presence here.

But these days will pass too quickly and next week we shall return to earth. For a time some of you will find the real world of home and parish, work or study, flat and disappointing.

Soon, too soon, you will all be going away. Briefly we are now here in Sydney at the centre of the Catholic world, but next week the Holy Father will return to Rome, we Sydneysiders will return to our parishes, while you, now visiting pilgrims, will go back to your homes in places near and far.

In other words during next week we shall be parting from one another. But when we part after these happy days, let us never part from our loving God and his Son Jesus Christ. And may Mary, Mother of God, whom we invoke in this World Youth Day as Our Lady of the Southern Cross, strengthen us in this resolution.

And so I pray:

Come, come O Breath of God, from the four winds, from all the nations and peoples of the earth and bless our Great South Land of the Holy Spirit. Empower us to be another great and immense army of humble servants and faithful witnesses. We make this prayer to God our Father in the name of Christ his Son. Amen.